THE
COLLEGE
SUCCESS
MANUAL

THE
COLLEGE
SUCCESS
MANUAL

HOW TO SUCCESSFULLY TRANSITION
FROM HIGH SCHOOL TO COLLEGE AND EARN A'S

DAVID S. LONG

dml Publishing LLC
Allen, Texas

Published by
dml Publishing LLC
Allen, Texas

Publisher's Cataloging-in-Publication Data
Long, David S.

The college success manual : how to successfully transition from high school to college and earn A's / David S. Long. – Allen, Tex. : dml Pub. LLC, 2011.

p. ; cm.

ISBN13: 978-0-9846444-0-7

1. Study skills--Handbooks, manuals, etc. 2. College student orientation--Handbooks, manuals, etc. 3. Academic achievement. I. Title.

LB2395.L66 2011
371.30281—dc22   2011932484

FIRST EDITION

Project coordination by Jenkins Group, Inc.
www.BookPublishing.com

Cover design by Chris Rhoads
Interior design by Brooke Camfield

Printed in the United States of America
15   14   13   12   11   •   5   4   3   2   1

Contents

Introduction   vii

Part One: Understanding the Importance of Organization   1
Process, content, and organization for college success
Organizing your college notebook
Why the college course syllabus is important
What a real college course syllabus looks like

Part Two: How to Be Successful in College   9
How to survive from day to day
Vital words and what professors mean when they use them

Part Three: Formal College Writing   21
Writing standards you must bring to college

Part Four: How to Write the Research Paper—Process   27
What your paper should physically look like
What your title page should look like
What source citation requirements you must meet
How you should use sic
What the thesis statement means to you
Recommended form for organizing the parts of your paper
Recommended form for making your research notes page
Checklist for reviewing the appearance of your paper

Part Five: How to Write the College Research Paper—Content   37

Steps to follow when researching your paper

Steps to follow when writing the content of your paper

Checklist for reviewing the content of your paper

Part Six: Writing the College Critique   47

Understanding the levels of appreciation

The college critique and what is expected of you

Recommended form for writing the college critique

Part Seven: Reading on the College Level   55

Becoming a more effective reader on the college level

Practical guide for reading your college assignments

Recommended form for taking reading notes

Part Eight: Your Professor—The Right Approach   59

How to approach your professor about a grade

What you should do when you disagree with your professor

How you should approach your professor's course evaluation

Index   63

Introduction

Congratulations on being accepted into college; it is quite an accomplishment! The next and most important hurdle you face, of course, is making a successful transition from high school student to college student. This is easier than most people think. After spending more than thirty years in the classroom, I have come to understand that the overwhelming numbers of students who do not do well in school suffer this fate for the same reason; they do not know how to do well! But learning how to do well is easy if you have the right guidance.

One of the saddest things that I witnessed during my teaching career was the sight of highly intelligent youngsters underperforming, and even failing, because they did not know how to learn in an academic environment. This manual addresses this issue. It is specifically designed to reduce your anxiety about college and to offer a practical step-by-step guide to show you how to be highly successful in college. The material contained herein will work if

The College Success Manual

you understand, appreciate, and apply its advice. In other words, study this manual and then take it to college with you and live it!

Remember that you were accepted into college because the admissions committee believed you could be successful. If it did not, your application for admission would have been denied. However, getting accepted into college is one thing; being successful and earning your degree is quite another.

This college manual is not intended to frighten you about college. On the contrary, my purpose is to open your eyes as to what is coming so that you can be better prepared to respond. The central experience in college is writing. If you do not know how to write on the college level, which includes the formal college research paper and the college critique, you are not going to be successful. This manual does not just tell you what should be done; it also shows you how to do it! As a result, you will hit the ground running when you start college instead of suffering, as too many freshman do, through weeks of adjustment and a lower GPA until you catch on to what is expected of you. An excellent time in your life is your college experience. Your parents and your community have prepared you for this unique and invaluable time in your life. Celebrate and embrace it! Armed with the advice and knowledge in this manual, you will have a college experience that is much more successful, more rewarding, and more enjoyable. I guarantee it. Let's get started.

Part One
Understanding the Importance of Organization

Three simple words—process, content, and organization—are the most important keys to being successful in college. Understanding and applying them effectively will bring you college success. Ignoring them will likely bring failure.

The Importance of Process

Unlike in high school, just getting the right answer in college is not good enough. How you present that correct answer to your professor is almost as important. Most professors, formally or informally, grade student assignments according to a formula, a common one being a 60/40 split. Sixty points out of 100 are available for the correct answer (content), and the remaining 40 points are available for the correct presentation of that answer (process). Let me give you an example to show why this is important. Suppose a student turns in an assignment that ignores process but is perfect with respect to its factual content. According to the formula, he or she would receive zero points for process and 60 points for content. What letter grade is a 60 percent?

What of the reverse situation? Now suppose a student turns in an assignment that is not content perfect but is process perfect. He or she receives, let us say, 48 points for content and all 40 points available for process. What letter grade is an 88? It is a grade of B+ (3.5 on a 4.0 college scale), which is good enough to be placed on the dean's list.

Do not fail to understand and to appreciate the important role that process plays in your college work. It could very well be the difference between succeeding in college and failing. Pay attention to how the professor wants his or her assignment organized and presented. Be particularly mindful of the technology revolution occurring on the college campus today and how it is changing the process rules for completing course requirements. Taking lecture and reading notes by laptop computer is becoming more common. The manner in which professor and student communicate with each other with respect to course syllabus, lectures, assignments, and exams is also under-going technological change. Two excellent examples of educational tools being utilized are *OneNote*, software by Microsoft, and BlackBoard, a multifunctional Web based program. Pay close attention when your professor explains the technology he or she will be requiring you to use to complete your course assignments and responsibilities. There are many process points available from your professors. Do not give them away. Go get them!

The Importance of Organization

I have witnessed countless students either underperform or fail outright because they could not find anything. These were highly intelligent students who were so disorganized and so cluttered in their student lives that they could only function minimally or not function at all. How could this be? The answer is to be found in the fact that they did not know any better! How can we blame a student in this performance situation if he or she has never been taught how and why to be organized? We cannot. You cannot learn in chaos, and this manual will show you how and why it is important to be organized.

How You Should Organize Your College Notebook

Due to the sheer volume of paper and documents a college student handles during each semester, I strongly recommend that a loose-leaf notebook be used instead of a spiral. Once paper is taken out of a spiral notebook, it cannot be returned. And stuffing the documents inside the book loose, or in its side pockets if they exist, only contributes to student disorganization and inefficiency.

Use a two-inch loose-leaf notebook for each course because papers can be removed and replaced with ease. Unless instructed otherwise by your professor, you should divide your course notebook into the following three distinct sections:

Section One: Class Notes

The first page of section one should be your professor's course syllabus. This document is extremely important because it tells you important things such as what books to buy, what assignments there are and when they are due, the philosophy and focus of the course, the professor's office hours and his or her contact numbers, and the course research and writing requirements. The professor will give you one copy. Do not lose it. Make a copy of all your course syllabi and store them in a safe place in case you do lose one. For a sample of what a college syllabus looks like, see page 6. Notice how the important course information is complete and detailed.

The rest of section one is college-lined paper for note taking. Remember to date your notes and keep them in chronological order. It is very common for a professor, at the end of a couple of weeks of lectures, to announce in class, "Quiz next time on lecture notes from September 4 through today." If you have not been dating your notes, how will you know what to study? Chronological organization of your lecture notes will also help you understand the connections the professor is making in the development of his or her course content. This is important for doing well on the course tests.

Although a majority of college students still use paper and pen, if you prefer to take your lecture and reading notes using a laptop or tablet PC, as mentioned earlier, *OneNote* by Microsoft is an excellent program that allows you to electronically organize your notes as I have recommended above.

Section Two: Assigned Readings

This section is where you place all assigned readings that come from your professor, your reading notes from an assigned textbook, a downloaded PDF file, or a copy of the document from your professor's reserved reading section in your college or university library. Make sure that all your required documents are there, that they are dated, and that the source of each document is fully cited. To cite a source, you need its title, author, publisher, and place and date of publication.

If a professor distributes a document in class that is not cited, immediately ask for the citation and write it on the document in a prominent place. It is important to do this every time you get your hands on a piece of paper. Why is this important? If you do not have a source citation for a document you may want to use in your research and writing, you cannot use the source. College students are always looking for more sources to use in their writing. What better place to look for sources when writing for a particular professor than the documents he or she has assigned? In addition, these scholarly sources will have relevant source citations of their own that can be consulted and possibly used.

Have a few pages of college-lined paper available immediately following each document for notes about the document taken from your professor, a class discussion, or your independent reading of it. (See page 56 for more specific guidance.)

Section Three: Grades

Save all graded assignments, tests, and quizzes given back to you by your professor in this section. College courses are cumulative. That is to say, they grow in detail and complexity as the semester unfolds. Work done later in a course is built upon work done earlier in the course. Monitoring your progress allows you not only to know how you are doing, but it also enables you to see the interconnectedness of the course material as it unfolds. As mentioned earlier, this interconnectedness is important for doing well on college tests. Remember, college tests are cumulative.

In addition, having all your work for a course stored in a safe place provides you with a complete answer to a professor inquiring about missing assignments. It allows you to show the graded assignment.

Remember: Never leave the only copies of your assignments saved on the hard drive of your computer. Crashes happen. Back up all files on a flash drive or burned to a CD.

Why the College Course Syllabus Is Important to You

At the first meeting of your college classes your professors will discuss their course syllabus. A syllabus is nothing more than an outline or summary of the main points of the course. Remember, this document is extremely important to your success in college. Whether it is distributed electronically or by paper copy, it is vitally important that you consult the course syllabus regularly.

If you refer to the following sample syllabus, you will very quickly understand why the syllabus is important. Among many other valuable pieces of information, such as what books to buy, what the philosophy and focus of the course are, what the professor's grading scale is, and what research and writing requirements there are, you will notice that specific assignments and their due dates are announced. Once you have received this announcement, you are on your own. It is now up to you to know where you have to be, when you have to be there, and what is expected of you. Do not show up late to class or unprepared. Your college professors are not going to hold your hand and lead you around. College is for adults. If you are not prepared to be one, go home.

On the following pages you will see part of a real college syllabus. Notice its specificity and importance. Without this vital course information students would be lost.

What a Real College Course Syllabus Looks Like

International Law
Gov. 127

Summer 2008   Dr. Peter J. Smith
Class Time: 6:20 – 8:20 p.m. TWR   Class room: BH18
Office: BH219   Phone: 365-9775
Office Hours: Mon. & Wed. 1:30 p.m. – 2:30 p.m.   Email: dlaw2.edu
Thurs. 5:00 p.m. – 6:00 p.m. (by appointment)

Course Overview

International Law is generally defined as the rules and principles governing the interaction among states. While some see international law as critical to the smooth progress of international relations, others see it as a set of moral principles that nations choose to obey or disobey at will. Yet others view the present system as part of the "colonial heritage" that must be altered to reflect changing needs. However, almost everyone agrees that international law is an inescapable part of life today. This course deals with areas of international law that make international relations a matter of course. We will study the legal principles that underlie such areas as the recognition of states, the rights and duties of a state, the extent of state jurisdiction over the individual, human rights and war crimes, and environmental protection.

Course Objectives

This course is designed to meet the following objectives:

1. To examine issues in international law that define the international system—the law of peace.

2. To develop legal thinking and writing by requiring students to (a) write two legal briefs on cases assigned in class, and (b) present an oral and written analysis of articles with the subject matter being discussed in class.

Credit

Three undergraduate semester hours

Required Readings

1. Malanczuk, Peter. 1997. *Akehurst's Modern Introduction to International Law.* Seventh Edition. New York: Rutledge.

2. Readings placed on reserve.

Criteria for Course Grade

Two legal briefs 50%

Final exam 20%

Case research and oral presentation 10%

Treaty analysis 20%

The first brief is due _____ and the second brief is due_____. These writing assignments may not be handed in late. In addition, students will select the dates they wish to present their case and treaty analysis. Students who are due to make the case presentation will submit three questions for class discussion to the instructor at least 24 hours before the class period to which they have been assigned. The questions arising from their assignment must be specific to the class but must be broad enough to generate discussion. The students are then responsible for being prepared to discuss any or all of the questions that they submit.

Reading Assignments

Week One

7/8	What Is International Law?	Chapters 1, 2
7/9	Sources of International Law	Chapters 3, 4
7/10	The Community of Nations	Chapters 5, 6

Week Two

7/15	Recognition of States and Government	Chapter 5
7/16	Rights of International Legal Persons	Chapter 8
7/18	Duties of State	Chapter 8

Week Three

7/22	Title to Territory	Chapters 10, 11, 13
7/23	Jurisdiction over Persons	Chapter 7
7/24	Extradition	Library reserve

Week Four

7/29	War Crimes and Tribunals	Library reserve
7/30	Human Rights Law	Chapter 14
7/31	Human Rights Law Continued	Chapter 14

Week Five

8/5	Environmental Law	Library reserve
8/6	Make-up Date	
8/7	Final Exam	

Part Two
How to Be Successful in College

Practical Advice on How to Survive from Day to Day

Make sure that you work hard so you not only graduate from college with a good GPA, but you also distinguish yourself enough to have the option of entering a good graduate school. A minimum grade-point average of a 3.0 (a B average) is required here. Doors of opportunity will open to you if you have a college grade-point average in the B range or better. Doors will close to you if you do not. Strive to earn A's; you have only eight semesters to do so. Here are some practical tips to help you become an excellent learner on the college level and to achieve a high GPA from the first day you enter college.

Put in the Time

Think of college as your full-time job. Put your full time into it! This takes real commitment and self-discipline. Unfortunately, many people are unable or unwilling to do this. How many hours per week is a typical full time job, thirty-five to forty? If you know what you are doing and are willing to put in a thirty-five or forty hour work week, you will graduate from college with a high grade-point average.

Manage Your Time

Do not wait for a convenient time to get to your studies. That time will never come! You must be proactive and attack your college work and get it behind you because more work is coming. Have a work schedule to organize your day. Schedule when you are attending classes, when you are going to work on particular course assignments, when you are going to study for a test, when you are going to eat, when you are going to bed and what time you are going to get up, and even when you are taking some time off for recreation. Chaos and poor performance will result if you do not have a plan and work that plan.

Avoid Employment during the School Year

Do not work during the school year unless you absolutely must. If you have to work to live and to put food on the table for you and your family, then by all means work. If not, work to earn the money for college during the summer months. You have to put a great deal of your time into your studies so do not be distracted. College is also more than just attending classes. Take advantage of the very many cultural activities of the college experience. It's tough to do this if you are working a job. Remember, school is your full-time job.

Get Your Rest

Remember what Ben Franklin taught us: "Early to bed and early to rise, makes a man healthy, wealthy, and wise." Believe it! If Franklin was correct, and he was, where would the opposite of his advice lead us? "Late to bed and late to rise, makes us sickly, poor, and dumb?" Watch your time-management during the school year. Do not adopt the destructive partying and sleeping habits of contemporary college life. You certainly want to enjoy your college years, but do not forget to be moderate in all things.

Never Miss Class

Never, ever miss a class and thereby take for granted the sacrifices you or your parents are going through to pay for your college education. You owe all those supporting you your honesty and your best efforts to get yourself educated.

Never Cut Class Because You Are Unprepared

Never cut a class because you are not prepared. Everyone drops the ball from time to time, and it is not the end of the world. But do not compound your problem by doing what children do: running away and hiding. Go to class even if unprepared. If the professor calls on you, be honest. Say, "Sorry, professor. I'm not prepared today, but I will be next time." Of course, make sure that the next time you are prepared because, as I have always done with my students in similar situations, you will probably be one of the first persons the professor calls upon to participate that day. Believe me, if you are prepared that day, you will gain the professor's respect. In fact, do not wait for the professor to call upon you; participate first.

Do the Work

Do all the work yourself, and stay away from study groups. Do not rely on fellow undergraduates to give you a college education; they are not competent to do so. If you are really struggling or at risk of failing in a subject, then by all means get extra help. Start with your professor. Giving extra help to students is part of his or her job. If you need extensive help, consult your college adviser for advice on obtaining competent professional tutoring. The last thing want to do is to trust your education to someone attempting to earn his or her first college degree.

Sit in the Front of Class

Always arrive early to class so you can sit in or near the front row. You will hear and see better than if you were in the back, and the professor will get to know you as an individual instead of just a number.

Be an Active Listener

Once the class has begun, actively listen also using your eyes. Yes, I said your eyes. I am amazed how many young people think they only listen with their ears. Listen with your eyes as well by watching the professor's lips. This may sound silly, but it works. See the words that come out of his or her mouth. You will be amazed at how much improved your listening and understanding will be. Your professors will also be impressed and feel complimented by your ability to focus and to pay attention. In our culture it is polite to look at the person speaking to you.

Remember, you do not learn anything by talking when the professor or someone else is speaking in class. You only learn when you actively listen. Acquire and apply the skill of silence.

Speak in Every Class

Ask or answer at least one legitimate question in every class. I do not mean speak to brown-nose the professor. That does not fool anyone and especially the professor. Ask and answer legitimate questions in class. To do this, of course, you must be prepared and be actively listening.

Establish a Respectful Relationship with Your Professors

Establish a friendly and respectful relationship with all your professors—and graduate assistants. Do not insult them by cutting their classes, especially before and after school holidays. This really upsets them, even if they tell you it does not. If you are going to miss a class for a legitimate reason, try to inform them prior to the class. If you are not able to do so, inform them as soon as possible before the next class. Do not give them the impression that you take them for granted. This will have a negative impact on your grade and harm you when you need letters of recommendation from your professors.

Review and Revise

The sooner you can get to review and to revise your notes from a particular class, the more you will understand and remember. The better your understanding, the better your grades will be. If possible, immediately after class find an empty classroom somewhere and read over and revise your notes. You did not write down everything the professor lectured about but, if you were actively listening, you heard everything. Now is the time to amend and to add to your notes. If you do so immediately after class, or as soon as your schedule permits, you will be amazed at how much additional relevant and important information you can add.

Read over all course notes at least once or twice a week. Do not wait until the night before or even a few days before a test to study your course notes. That is too late, and you will be flirting with disaster. College exams, essays especially, ask for big-picture analyses. Professors want to see that you understand the interconnection of things. They want you to demonstrate that you understand the entire picture as they have presented it to you. You cannot demonstrate this unless you have been paying attention to the unfolding or development of the professor's material, which should be reflected in your course notes.

Attack Your Assignments

Try to start all assignments on the day they are assigned. Be proactive here. This is particularly critical when dealing with research papers. Have a schedule of when things are due and take charge of your education. As stressed earlier, do not wait for a convenient time to get to your assignments because that time will never come. If you want a college degree, you have to go get it.

Reading

The purpose of reading is to understand. When a professor assigns a reading, you are not just being asked to read the material once. You are being asked to understand it. No one reads everything and understands it the first time. We all have to reread material. Understand and accept this. Make certain that when you read an assignment, it is completely understood. If not, read it again. Never skip over words you do not understand. Consult your college dictionary and, when out and about on campus or in class, carry and use a pocket electronic dictionary.

Writing

The purpose of writing is to be understood. Proof your work to make certain that you have written exactly what you want to convey. Say what you mean and mean what you say. Do you understand you? If not, your professors will probably not either, and your grades will suffer. Remember that important lesson about writing from Blaise Pascal. After he wrote a very lengthy letter to a friend, he ended it with the phrase, "I have made this letter longer than usual, only because I have not had time to make it shorter." Good writing takes time and effort.

Struggle

College is supposed to be a time of growth. It will be for you if you do what is required to be successful—struggle! Personal growth and improvement comes from facing adversity, not running away from it. When you are confronted with difficult college assignments, do not run away from them. Face them and fight your way to mastery. Remember how the on-deck baseball batter is attempting to improve his next performance at the plate; he is struggling by swinging a heavier bat.

Work Ethic

Work is not something to be avoided or, if unavoidable, to be completed quickly and with a minimum of effort. Work is good for you. You should like to work. It is, indeed, in many ways its own reward. Embrace a strong work ethic. Developing discipline, conscientiousness, and a strong work ethic is at the center of what a successful college career, and quite frankly a successful life, is all about.

Remember that you have the rest of your life to sleep, to goof off, to play poker or to party, but you only have one chance at a college education. Do not fail to take full advantage of your opportunity. Work hard so you have no regrets about your college years. Graduate with distinction.

It has been estimated that approximately thirty out of every one hundred high school graduates successfully complete college. And only some of those graduating from college go on to graduate school. Make certain you are one of those few. The shortest distance from poverty to wealth in America is education. The average income of the college graduate is estimated to be 60 percent higher than the average income of the high school graduate. There are plenty of statistics that suggest that the college graduate lives longer, enjoys a higher quality of life, and earns, over a working career, more than two times than the non-graduate.

Remember Who You Are

Remember that you do not come from the moon. What you are and what you have accomplished thus far comes from what your parents, your teachers, and your community have given to you. Do not fail to appreciate and to remember this point. When you are educated, and in a position to do so, turn around and help someone else make it. We are all connected and part of one of the greatest countries in the world. Support education and remember it is not a liability but an investment. It is a citizen responsibility and not just a parent responsibility. Society is made better when its members are well educated. You have your life in your hands, so keep a good grip on it!

Vital Words and What Professors Mean When They Use Them

Literal: Said directly or word for word.

> The sky is blue.
> You must do all my work to pass my class.
> You can't go to the movies tonight.

The above statements are literal expressions. There is no confusion about their meaning because the information is presented directly. When you hear professors use terms like express (as in "express language") or explicit (as in "explicit language"), they mean literal.

When you hear a professor ask "What is the denotation of that term?" you are asked to tell the literal meaning of that term. Remember, the words denotation, literal, explicit, and express all mean the same thing.

Implied: Said indirectly, or not word for word. To understand what is implied, you must, as the saying goes, read between the lines. What would you guess if someone told you that there was a great deal of black smoke coming from inside your house? Would you think fire? Of course you would. But did that person use the word fire? No, it was implied. When meaning is sent indirectly, not expressly, explicitly, or literally, it is being implied. When you attempt to understand meaning, as in the above case, you are drawing an inference. An inference is a guess or a conclusion as to what is meant because the meaning has not been sent literally. Remember, senders of meaning imply, while receivers of meaning infer. When the professor asks what inferences can be drawn from a particular reading, you are being asked to identify what the author is implying.

Simile: Direct or literal comparison using like or as. "Life is like a box of chocolates." This is a direct (or literal, explicit, or express) comparison between a box of chocolates and life. Remember, explicit, express, and literal all mean the same thing.

Metaphor: Indirect or implied comparison.

> The woman gave her husband an icy glance.
> The candidate had a highly effective war room.
> She has nerves of steel.
> The journey my business took last fiscal year was successful.

It is said that a picture is worth a thousand words. Well, in a very real sense the metaphor gives us a mental picture that enhances or improves our understanding. Their use shows how things or categories of things relate to one another in ways that would be more difficult to understand or to explain otherwise.

Ambiguous: Subject to more than one meaning or interpretation.

> Mary, if you come to class late again, I am going to take action.
> No person may be deprived of property without due process of law.
> Criminal law is based on an eye for an eye and a tooth for a tooth.

All of the above statements are ambiguous. Many things could happen to Mary; we just don't know what for sure. What must a person go through before losing his or her property? Again, we are not sure. Does "an eye for an eye" mean revenge? Does it mean that the punishment must fit the crime? Again, we are faced with ambiguity.

Appreciation: To assign value (does not mean thank you).

You are walking to your college apartment when you notice a friend attempting to carry six bags of groceries to her apartment, which is up three flights of stairs. You help her and at the end she says, "Thanks very much for your help; I really appreciate it." What is she literally saying to you? She is not saying thank you twice, is she? She is saying that she values what you have done for her.

When you buy a new car and drive it off the dealer's lot, what is happening to the value of that new car? Yes, it is depreciating, or going down in value. When you buy a home in a nice neighborhood and take good care of it, what usually happens over time to the value of your house? Yes, it appreciates, or increases, in value.

Appreciation is a term that is very important to you and will be discussed in greater detail later when the college critique is explained.

Polemics: Arguments, controversies, or disputes usually associated with social comment or criticism.

During your college career you will be exposed to all sorts of opposing views that are usually associated with criticism of society and how to make it better. Editorial and opinion writers of newspapers engage in polemics all the time. So do public speakers and authors of books and essays.

Polemicists are more common than you think. When Martin Luther nailed his ninety-five theses to the church door and started the Protestant Reformation, he was criticizing Catholic religious society in an attempt to make it better. He was engaging in polemics.

Karl Marx was engaging in polemics (social criticism) when he wrote *The Communist Manifesto*. Martin Luther King, Jr. was making a profound polemic of contemporary American society and its system of legal segregation when he wrote *Letter from Birmingham City Jail*. Abraham Lincoln offered a polemic when he spoke about our nation not being half slave and half free. Polemics are all around us.

Style manual: Process rules for the design and writing of documents.

Not all professors require the same manual. How you cite the source will vary depending on the requirements of your professor. Be sure to consult the required style manual for the correct citation form.

Source citation: Telling what sources you have used in your paper.

If you use the words or ideas of others in your paper, you must cite (tell) their source. Remember that taking the words of someone else but changing them into your own words (paraphrasing) still requires you to cite the source. All direct quotes and paraphrases must be cited.

Part Three

Formal College Writing

Writing Standards You Must Bring to College

A great deal of your college experience will center on research, writing, reading, and critiquing. When you arrive at college, your professors will expect you to know how to do all of these things reasonably well. No one is going to baby-sit you or hold your hand. You are either competent to be successful in college from day one, or you are in for a very difficult time.

What follows are the minimum college writing standards you must meet to have any chance of getting off to a successful start. Unless instructed otherwise for a given assignment, your college writing should be formal. All of your writing should conform to these guidelines.

- **Do not use contractions:** Contractions, such as shouldn't, couldn't, it's, and don't, are informal language. College writing is mostly formal.

- **Do not use the personal pronoun "I":** If you must refer to yourself in your writing, use the phrase "in the view of this writer." Use of "I" is permissible, however, only if writing a personal narrative.

- **Do not use the phrase "in my opinion":** Use of this phrase may suggest tentativeness or lack of conviction, and you are already expressing your opinion when writing.

- **Do not use "etc":** If you have something to say, say it. If you do not have anything additionally to say, either find something or shut up. Do not bluff. It does not fool anyone.

Check your grammar and spelling:

Relying on your computer's spelling and grammar program is not enough. For example, if you meant "use" but wrote "us," the computer will not recognize any error. Always personally read through your material to ensure that it is free of errors and reflects exactly what you want to say.

Pronoun and its antecedent must always agree: If the antecedent to the pronoun is singular, then the pronoun must be singular. If the antecedent to the pronoun is plural, then the pronoun must be plural.

Which is correct?

    A. Everyone must do their homework.

    B. Everyone must do his or her homework.

Is everyone singular or plural? It is singular because it refers to every one. Therefore, the pronoun must be singular. Choice B is grammatically correct.

Which is correct?

    A. All students brought their books to class.

    B. All students brought his or her books to class.

Is all singular or plural? It is plural because it is referring to more than one. Therefore the pronoun must be plural. Choice A is grammatically correct.

Note: This is such a common mistake today that some experts will lead to you believe that the "modern" way is to use their in all cases. I can assure you that your college English professors will not be so modern.

Be careful of the tone of your writing: Be sensitive to the tone of your writing and the effect or impression it will have on your professors who are reading and grading it. Remember that the first duty of a writer is to be understood. Do not write to impress or to show how many big vocabulary words you know. "Keep it simple stupid" (KISS) is good advice for all of us to follow when writing.

Be polite in your writing: Always be polite and show respect. It should be Mr., Ms., former President Bush, Governor Perry, former governor Cuomo and not Bush, Perry, or Cuomo. If you want to reference people who are no longer alive, then it is not impolite to refer to them using only their last name. For instance, Kennedy, Lincoln, Roosevelt.

The weight of words: Let words speak of their own weight. Do not use emphasis unless you have a very good reason for doing so. Avoid attempting to raise the volume of words through the use of italics, bold, capitalization, or underlining. If you absolutely need to emphasize words contained within a quotation, make certain that you announce within the quotation that you have done so. The following example demonstrates how this is done:

> I am convinced that President Reagan is a man *I can do business with* (emphasis added) and I am going to take a chance on him.

Do not mix tenses: If you are writing about something or someone in the past, you must be in the past tense. If you are writing about something or someone in the present, you must be in the present tense.

When writing about Abraham Lincoln, for instance, you could not say "he writes"; it must be "he wrote." You could not say "he says"; it must be "he said." You could not say "he believes"; it must be "he believed." This is done, of course, because Lincoln is in the past.

When writing about something or someone in the present, you must be in the present tense. President Bush "believes," not President Bush "believed." President Bush "states," not President Bush "stated."

If, however, the person you are writing about changes his or her views and now believes or argues something different, then use of the past tense would be appropriate when writing about those changed views or arguments. For example, President Bush "believed" there were WMD in Iraq. He now believes differently.

The important thing to remember here is to be careful that you do not unintentionally mix your tenses. Pay attention and be consistent throughout your writing.

Common Mistakes with Confusing Words

	Examples
Their, there, and they're	
Their: Pronoun (shows ownership)	The children packed their books.
There: Adverb (place or introductory word)	Put your books over there. There are 28 kids in the class.
They're: Contraction for *they are*	They're coming to dinner.
Its, It's	
Its: Possessive pronoun	The cat licked its paws.
It's: Contraction for it is	It's time to leave.

Than, Then

Than: Comparison	Kim is taller than Jim.
Then: Adverb meaning *point in time* or *therefore*	Then I will speak.

To, Too, Two

To: Preposition/infinitive	Go to the store for me. He wants to tell his mom.
Too: Also/excessively	I ate too much cake. I too want to swim today.
Two: Number	I ate two hamburgers.

Whose, who's

Whose: Possessive pronoun	Whose books are on the floor?
Who's: Contraction for *who is*	Who's coming home with you?

Note: If you do not use contractions in your formal college writing, you will not have to deal with the contraction mistakes discussed above.

Important Prefixes and Suffixes You Should Remember

Inter-: Between	International law is the law between nations. Interstate commerce is business between states.
Intra-: Within	Intrastate commerce is business within a single state. Intrastate vehicle regulations apply only within the state.

-ism: Belief or an idea	Communism, Capitalism, Marxism, Chauvinism, Romanticism
-ist: Person who believes in an idea	Communist, Capitalist, Marxist, Chauvinist

Correlative Conjunction (Neither/nor and either/or)

Neither goes with *nor,* and *either* goes with *or.* Although they may all be used individually, no other pairing is correct.

For example:

> Neither John nor Mary has ridden a horse before today.
> Either I will go on vacation next week or wait and go in two weeks.

Use of Numbers

When using numbers in your writing, spell out numbers one through nine and spell out hundreds, thousands, millions, and billions, and so on. This means that only part of some numbers will be written out. For example:

> nine million, 10 thousand, 50 million, six thousand, eight billion

Ordinal Numbers

Spell out all ordinal (order) numbers under one hundred. For example: first, second, fifteenth, twenty-fourth.

Part Four

How to Write the College Research Paper—Process

What Your Paper Should Physically Look Like

Unless your professor tells you otherwise, your research paper should conform to the following process rules:

- **Type size and font:** Use twelve-point type and Times New Roman font.

- **Margins:** Margins are one inch on the top/bottom/left/right of each page.

- **Justification:** If your professor wants you to both left- and right-justify your paper, be sure to use one space after each comma and each period. This will eliminate extra spacing in the text. If your professor does not state a preference, left and right justify your paper. This looks better.

- **Indenting:** All new paragraphs should be indented five spaces by hitting the Tab key once.

- **Block quoting:** If you use quotations that are longer than five double-spaced lines in your paper, you must block the quotation. You cannot double-space a long quote. You will be criticized for filling, and your grade will suffer. All block quotes are indented on both sides, single-spaced, and justified.

- **Source citation:** If you use the words or ideas of others in your paper, you must cite (tell) what the source is. How you cite the source will vary depending on the requirements of your professor. Be sure to consult the required style manual for the correct citation form.

   What the professor requires should be on his or her course syllabus. If it is not, publicly ask the professor which style manual is required and write it down on your syllabus.

- **Sources:** Use a variety of sources (mostly scholarly journals). Do not use dictionaries or encyclopedias; they are too general and are not considered scholarly enough for college-level research. If necessary, they can be used to quickly bring you up to speed on a given topic.

   As a general rule, you should strive to have one source for each page of required length. This does not mean that you should necessarily have a source on each page. However, for a ten-page paper to have a chance to be any good, strive to have ten different sources. For a twenty-page paper, try to have twenty sources. Falling short one or two sources is not fatal.

- **Page numbering:** There is to be no page numbering on the title page, page one, or the bibliography or reference pages. Start page numbering with page two of the text of your paper, and end it on the last page of text. Page numbers should be centered on the bottom of each page.

- **Title page (upper half of page):** Titles of papers are centered in the top half of the paper. On standard size paper, hit

Enter ten times and then center your title. Major words of titles are capitalized; minor words are not. Either underline or italicize all titles throughout your paper, and do not mix them. For example:

What Role Should the Federal Government
Play in Regulating the Economy?

or

<u>What Role Should the United States Play</u>
<u>in Regulating the Economy?</u>

- **Title page (lower half of page)**: Student identifying information is centered on each line on the lower half of the page. On standard size paper, hit Enter an additional twenty times from the end of the title and then type your information. Remember, the only place your name appears on your paper is on the title page. See page 30 for a model of what the title page should look like.

Miscellaneous

1. No plastic covers!

2. Use one staple in the top left corner.

3. No pictures in your paper unless required to advance your thesis.

4. Use tables, charts, and graphs to advance your thesis.

5. Make sure to explain how the data advances your thesis.

6. Make sure the data is large enough to be read easily, but not so large that you will be criticized by your professor for filling.

*What Role Should the Federal Government
Play in Regulating the Economy?*

Name of your college or university
Your name
Course title and number
Professor's name
Paper's due date

What Source Citation Requirements You Must Meet

It is perfectly permissible for you to take the words or ideas of others and put them into your research paper. In fact, your professors will want and expect you to do so. If you use the words or ideas of someone else, you must announce in your paper where and from whom it was taken. Such an announcement is called a source citation. How you cite the sources is determined by the required style manual. Failure to do so is plagiarism and, depending on how serious the cheating is, could very well result in you being expelled from college.

A style manual is a set of process rules for the design and writing of your documents for submission or publication. There are many types of style manuals used in college, and not all professors require the same manual because different disciplines require different process rules. Some of the more common style manuals include the *American Political Science Association* (APSA), the *American Psychology Association* (APA), *Modern Language Association* (MLA), the *Chicago Manual of Style* (CMS), the *American Anthropological Association* (AAA), and the *Council of Science Editors* (CSE). Consult the Web to review and to download detailed explanations of any given style manual.

How You Should Use *Sic*

What do you do when you want to quote writers in your research paper but they have made a spelling or grammatical error? Do you fix or repeat the mistake? If you repeat the mistake, how can you ensure that the professor will not mark you down because he or she believes that you made the mistake?

You cannot change a person's words when quoting them and so therefore you must repeat the mistake. But to announce that the mistake lies with the author of the quote and not you, you must use *sic*.

Sic (Latin for *thus*) is used in quotations to indicate that you have quoted the material exactly as it appeared in the original work. Sic is placed within brackets and in lowercase letters. Look at each example below to see how you should identify an error using *sic*.

In *Basic Astronomy,* Professor Murphy stated that "the earth does not revolve around the son [*sic*] at the same rate of speed."

President Roosevelt stated clearly that "the only thing we have to feare [*sic*] is fear itself."

President Kennedy stated on more than one occasion that "their [*sic*] is a great deal of risk to our continuing involvement in Vietnam."

What the Thesis Statement Means to You

Now that you have selected the topic of your research paper, you must think about a thesis statement. A thesis statement is the main idea or focus of your paper. The thesis statement cannot be overemphasized. If you do not have one, you are wasting your valuable time. Do not attempt to research blind. A thesis statement is simple and can take different forms, such as:

1. A thesis statement can be a question.

   Example: *What form of government did the Founding Fathers choose for our country?*

   Your research paper could then answer this question.

2. A thesis statement may require you to make an argument.

   Example: *The United States should withdraw from the UN.*

   Your research paper could either prove or disprove this thesis.

3. A thesis statement may compare and or contrast two or more things.

   Example: *The health care system in the U.S. is better than in Japan.*

   Your research paper could discuss how the two health care systems compare (are the same) as well as contrast (how they are different) as part of your assessment of the quality of each.

Recommended Form for
Organizing the Parts of Your Paper
(CD Form #1)

Do not waste your valuable time with blind research. Complete this form before you spend any serious research time and bring it with you to the library.

What is your thesis?

_____

What are the subsections of your thesis, and how many pages are you devoting to each?

Part One: _____ Pages _____

Part Two: _____ Pages _____

Part Three: _____ Pages _____

Add one page (three paragraphs)
for your introduction   Pages _____

Add one page (two to three paragraphs)
for your conclusion   Pages _____

                                                    Total pages_____

Note: Use the above formula for a paper of ten to fifteen pages. For a paper that is more than ten pages, consider adding or lengthening sections.

Recommended Form for Taking Your Research Notes
(CD Form #2)

Number _____ Part _____ TopicRelevance _____

Part One: Source citation information

Author _____

Title _____

Publisher _____

Date published _____

Place published _____

Part Two: Information summary (quotes and paraphrasing)

_____

_____

_____

_____

_____

_____

_____

_____

_____

_____

Note: Do not reshelf materials until you have filled in the information required in Part One above.

Checklist for Reviewing the Appearance of Your Paper
(CD Form #3)

Review the physical appearance of your completed paper to make sure you have met the requirements listed below:

_____ 8.5 x 11 white paper

_____ One-inch margins

_____ Times New Roman

_____ Type size 12

_____ Double-spaced

_____ Blocked quotes singled-spaced and indented

_____ Title page

_____ Your name appears only on your title page

_____ No plastic cover

_____ One staple in upper left corner

_____ No pictures (unless forced by thesis)

_____ No contractions (except what may be in a quote)

_____ Checked for spelling and grammatical mistakes

_____ All data, charts, and graphs explained

_____ All sources of direct quotes (words) cited

_____ All sources of paraphrasing (ideas) cited

_____ The paper is neat and clean

Part Five

How to Write the College Research Paper—Content

Steps to Follow When Researching Your Paper

1. **Pick your topic:** Unless the professor specifically chooses the topic for you, do general background reading on a topic that you like. Write down things about the topic you would like to know more about. Whatever the paper's assigned length, the process of researching and writing is the same.

2. **You must have a thesis for your paper:** Do not begin any detailed research without first deciding on a thesis or main purpose of your paper. If you do not, you are researching blind and therefore wasting your valuable time. (See page 32 for a detailed explanation of the thesis statement.)

3. **Organize your paper and assign length to its parts:** Depending on the required length of you paper, divide your thesis into content parts. Ten-page papers and less are usually divided into three content parts. For example, part one could be arguments in support of your thesis; part two

could be arguments in opposition to your thesis; and part three could offer your personal view.

If your paper requirement is greater than ten pages, you could lengthen each part or add more parts. Remember, when calculating how long each part has to be to meet your professor's required length, you need one page (three paragraphs) for your introduction and one to two pages for your conclusion. See page 34 for the recommended form to use when outlining the organization of your paper.

4. **Time to build your paper:** Now is the time to research and to write the parts of your paper. Remember, research papers are built. You never write ten, fifteen, or more pages on anything. Research papers consist of mini essays put together to make a multipage paper. Just research and write your content parts and then piece the paper together. Add on your introduction, conclusion, and source citation page (if required), and you are done.

Lower any anxiety you may have about writing your first formal college research paper by remembering something very important. It is not necessary, or even possible, to say everything there is to say about your topic. The only thing that is necessary is that you say enough. What is enough? For a ten-page paper, ten pages are enough. For a fifteen-page paper, fifteen pages are enough. Relax and follow the step-by-step guide that I have provided.

5. **Collect facts and build your paper's source base:** Consult a whole variety of sources. Your paper will only be as good as the sources you use! Primary sources (original works) are better than secondary sources, although there is nothing wrong with secondary sources. Current sources are generally preferable to older sources, so watch the copyright dates. Do not source dictionaries or encyclopedias in your paper, and never use newspapers exclusively. Again, variety is important.

On the recommended form for research note taking (see pages 35), record researched ideas that directly relate to your thesis parts that you think you can use. Be sure to document your sources as the form advises so you have all the information necessary to fully cite them when the time comes. There is nothing worse than having good sources that cannot be used because you neglected to write down the necessary sourcing information.

It is important to make sure to balance the total number of your sources. Too few sources and you will be criticized for writing a paper that is too general and lacking in specifics. Too many sources and you will be criticized for not putting enough of your own ideas into the paper. For a ten page paper, using from eight to twelve sources is appropriate.

6. **Organize your thoughts:** Read through all your research notes and sort them by relevance to your content parts. Place them in the order you wish to present them in your paper.

7. **Write your paper:** Follow the steps concerning the introduction, body, and conclusion of all effective papers discussed on pages 40 through 44. Do not pressure yourself and allow enough time for several drafts. Complete your paper at least one week before it is due. This gives you ample time to fix things that may arise such as computer or printer failure, factual mistakes, or a new and valuable source you want to add to your paper. Good things happen when you start and finish your paper early. Bad things happen when you wait until the last minute.

8. **Double-check facts and proofread:** As mentioned earlier, proof your work for spelling and grammatical errors twice. Have your computer program scan for errors first and then personally read and check for errors. Remember, your

computer scan will not see anything wrong with "there" if you meant "their."

Use the recommended checklist forms to verify that your completed paper has met all the process and content requirements. Do not forget to also check that you have met any additional or different requirements from your professor.

Steps to Follow When Writing the Content of Your Paper

All effective formal college research papers have three distinct parts: the introduction, the body, and the conclusion. Each part has steps or requirements that must be met. What follows is a detailed explanation of those requirements:

Introduction

What is supposed to happen in the introduction? Let me illustrate by telling you the following story:

> Once upon a time, Farmer Mike wanted to sell his prize mule. Farmer Bill from a neighboring farm came to see it. Farmer Mike told Farmer Bill that he loved his mule. "He doesn't overeat; he works from sunrise to sunset without complaint; you don't have to abuse him. Just treat him with love and kindness. My kids just love him."
>
> Farmer Bill was impressed and asked how much Farmer Mike wanted for him. When he was told one thousand dollars, Farmer Bill said, "That's a lot of money for a mule." Farmer Mike responded, "Yes, but that's a lot of mule, and you won't be sorry."
>
> Farmer Bill paid the asking price and took the mule to his farm. First thing in the morning Farmer

Bill hooked the mule to the plow and said, "Let's go and do a good day's work." The mule didn't move. Farmer Bill kindly encouraged the animal to move once more. The mule didn't move. After a third try failed, Farmer Bill thought he smelled a rat. He immediately called Farmer Mike, told him of his trouble, and insisted that he come to his farm and either fix the problem or give him his money back. Farmer Mike said he would be right over.

After Farmer Mike arrived at Farmer Bill's farm, he went around behind Farmer Bill's barn and found a six-foot-long two-by-four. He then went back to the animal and, without hesitation, cracked the wood over its head. "There, that should do it" said Farmer Mike. "Problem solved."

Shocked beyond belief, Farmer Bill said, "What in the world are you doing? I thought you told me that this animal was a great and cooperative worker and that all I needed to do was to show it love and kindness." Farmer Mike smiled and said, "Yes, all of that is true. This is a wonderful animal, but first you have to get its attention."

That, ladies and gentlemen, is what the very first part of your introduction should do. Get the attention of your audience by breaking a piece of lumber over their heads! Do not start your paper by just talking about your topic.

Step One: The Attention Step (First Paragraph)

Get the attention of your audience in a way that is directly related to your thesis. Here are the four ways to do it:

1. Use a shocking or provocative statement.

2. Use poetry or lyrics from a song.

3. Use a dramatic or profound quotation.

4. Use wit or humor.*

* Be careful with choice four above. Make sure it works. There is nothing worse than a failed attempt at wit or humor.

Step Two: First Summary (Second Paragraph)

Tell your audience what you are going to do. Now remember, you are no longer in seventh grade, so avoid the phrase, "In my paper I am going to talk about…" Teachers get nauseated when they see that phrase, so do not use it! Be more sophisticated in your presentation. Use phrases like, "The following presentation will address . . ." or "This presentation will speak to the issue of . . ." or "Let us examine . . ."

Step Three: Need or Hook Step (Third Paragraph)

With respect to your topic, tell your audience why it is important that they read your presentation. What's in it for them? In other words, "hook them," pique their curiosity to where they feel they must read your work. Do not use the phrase, "You should read my paper because it will be good for you and you will learn something," or something similar. Do not insult the intelligence of your audience.

How Long Should the Introduction Be?

The introduction consists of three paragraphs only. Paragraph one gets the attention of your audience in a way that advances or is directly related to your thesis. Paragraph two briefly announces what the paper is about. Paragraph three hooks your audience into wanting to read your paper. Try to limit your introduction to one full page of text and no more.

Body

The body of your paper consists of two required parts. First, begin by making a smooth (relevant) transition from the introduction. Use rhetorical questions here (questions you ask and intend to answer). Using subtitles can also be effective, as is the phrase "Let us begin by . . ."

In the second part of the body, do exactly what you announced you would do in paragraph two of your introduction. Do nothing more and nothing less than what you said you were going to do.

Conclusion

Part One: Final Summary

The conclusion consists of two required parts. First, give a final summary of the main ideas expressed in your paper. Do not add any new information here. You are just summarizing what you said in the body of your paper. Again, you are not in seventh grade, so avoid the phrase, "In my paper I said that . . ." Phrases such as "So we have seen that . . ." or "This presentation has dealt with . . ." are much better and are recommended.

Part Two: Action Step

The second part of the conclusion is what I call the action step. Now that you gave your audience the content of your paper, what do you want them to do with it? Tell them. Do not just end your paper by stopping. You need what the English teachers tell us is a clincher. Depending on the thesis of your paper, you may want them to take action as a citizen, write a letter to their elected officials, or protest in the streets, or continue to be informed as a responsible citizen and join in on the public debate.

Write the Introduction Last

Wait until you have written the content parts of your paper before you write your introduction. If you do, you will have a greater understanding of the topic of your paper and therefore be in a much better position to write a more effective introduction. Remember, papers are pieced together, so it does not matter which parts you write first. Start with content part one and finish it. Then go on to part two and finish that. Based on what you have learned from researching and writing parts one and two, you are now in the best position, if this is your paper's organization, to write part three, which is a highly informed personal view. Write the conclusion next and then, finally, write your introduction.

Write a More Effective Introduction

As discussed in detail on page 40, the introduction consists of three parts, with each part having a specific purpose. Paragraph one is the attention step, and there are four ways suggested to gain your reader's attention. You can acquire material for this step by remembering that all effective papers are speeches that have been reduced to writing. Yes, speeches.

For material to gain your reader's attention, consult speech and joke books. Whenever writing or preparing to give a speech, I consult a variety of sources for my introduction. One is the *Complete Speaker's and Toastmaster's Library*, by Jacob M. Braude. It is a multivolume work containing such titles as *Human Interest Stories*; *Speech Openers and Closers*; *Origins and Firsts*; *Rhyme and Verse—To Help Make a Point*; and *Proverbs, Epigrams, Aphorisms, Sayings and Bon Mots*.

You do not have to come up with original ways to gain your reader's attention. If I read a dramatic story or quotation that impresses me in a newspaper or magazine, I clip it and save it in my files for future use. There are plenty of resources available to you if you are observant. As a college student, be alert to this and start your own files. Of course, always remember to write down the citation information so you can use the source.

Checklist for Reviewing the Content of Your Paper
(CD Form #4)

Review the parts of your completed paper to make sure you have met the required steps listed below:

Introduction (Three Paragraphs)

_____ Did you get the attention of your audience?

_____ Did you tell them what you are going to do?

_____ Did you hook them into wanting to read your paper?

Body

_____ Did you do exactly what you said you would do in paragraph two (initial summary) of your introduction?

Conclusion

_____ Did you summarize what you wrote in part one of your paper?

_____ Did you summarize what you wrote in part two of your paper?

_____ Did you clinch, or bring your paper to a clear end?

Part Six
Writing the College Critique

You Must Understand the Levels of Appreciation

There are three distinct levels of appreciation, and you must understand all of them. Doing so will give you an extremely valuable frame of reference for making qualitative assessments or judgments about the work of other scholars. Assessing, comparing, contrasting, applying, and judging the work of scholars is a primary task of the college student and emerging intellectual. What are the three levels, and how are they different from one another? A description with an example of each level illustrating the difference follows.

Level One: Basic Level of Appreciation

The first level of appreciation is the basic. This is where the person is experiencing something for the first time. He or she has no prior experience or intellectual investment with a given activity. Let me illustrate using a music example. A person on the basic level of appreciation attending a philharmonic orchestra concert for the first time, when asked to critique the performance by giving his or her reactions to it, might say such things as, "I liked how the orchestra played loud and soft." Or, "The ladies looked beautiful in their black gowns." Or, "Wow! The orchestra had nine string bass players. What a powerful sound!" Or, "The drummer's hands moved fast."

As you can see, the person's lack of knowledge and experience with the philharmonic necessarily limits the specifics or intellectual depth of his or her remarks. This is not a criticism of the person but merely a reflection of the quality of a person's knowledge of a given activity.

Level Two: Intellectual Level of Appreciation

A person who has some prior experience and some learning relating to a given activity has made an intellectual investment. If a person on the intellectual level of appreciation for orchestral music (someone who plays the violin or took music appreciation in school, for example), went to the same philharmonic concert mentioned above, his or her performance reactions would be different. He or she might say such things as, "The string section had some difficulty with the uniformity of their bowing, and it flattened the performance." Or, "The percussionist missed two five-stroke roll releases in the second movement." Or, "The concertmaster did an excellent job in her solo; her vibrato was brilliant."

As you can see, the person's prior experience and knowledge of the philharmonic activity is clearly reflected in his or her critique of the orchestra's performance. It demonstrates firsthand knowledge and experience.

Level Three: Critical Level of Appreciation

The highest level of appreciation is the critical. This is where the person is the expert in a given field of endeavor. This person not only has the experience and intellectual investment described above, but has possibly also written the books, taught the courses, and actively participated in the activity.

If a person on the critical level of appreciation attended the same philharmonic concert describe above, his or her critique of the performance might include such comments as, "The conductor had a successful night. The orchestra correctly interpreted Bach's first movement." Or, "The middle kettle drum was out of tune by a half step." Or, "The concert master misinterpreted Mozart's notes with respect to the second movement."

As you can see, this expert critique is highly technical and reflective of a great depth of knowledge and experience.

I discuss the levels of appreciation with you not only because it is a valuable and crucial frame of reference for writing a highly effective college critique, but it is also an excellent reference for assessing the quality of everything. Yes, everything. For example, it is instructive, when listening to a speaker on a given subject, to judge on what level—basic, intellectual, or critical—is the speaker's knowledge. It is also valuable to have a good idea on what level you find your professor, your doctor, your clergy, and even your insurance salesperson.

The College Critique and What Is Expected of You

The college critique is a high-level critical-thinking activity and, after the formal college research paper, represents the second most important college writing assignment. When you are assigned by your professor to critique a book, a journal article, a speech, or any other intellectual work, you are being asked to evaluate it and to assign it value. In other words, you are being asked to appreciate it on the critical level.

For instance, what does the piece mean to you? Do you like it? Why or why not? With what do you agree or disagree?

How does the thesis (main idea) of the work of Professor Jones compare and contrast with the work of Professor Peters? How relevant is the thesis of Mr. Bloomberg to today's modern society? The form a critique assignment may take can differ widely. Be flexible and give the professor exactly what he or she wants; nothing more and nothing less.

Critiques do not usually require source citation or a works-cited page. If you do use outside sources, then you must cite them inside your critique. They also do not usually require a title page or page numbering. However, they are always of a required length and require you to do more than one intellectual activity.

If your professor assigns a critique but gives you no other instruction other than "write me a three-page critique," then I strongly recommend that you adopt the following critique format.

Page One: Objective Summary

Give an objective summary of what the author's piece is about. What did they author say? Do not editorialize in this part. Summarize it as if you were explaining it to someone who had not read it. Do not run over onto the second page. If you do, cut it back to one full page.

Page Two: Identifying Ideas of Agreement

Identify and briefly explain two ideas of the author with which you agree.

Page Three: Identifying Ideas of Disagreement

Identify and briefly explain two ideas of the author with which you disagree.

Note: On the following three pages you will find what this critique format should physically look like. The X's represent what your words might be. Use this format unless the professor instructs otherwise. If the professor assigns a six-page critique with no other instructions, consider doubling this recommended format. Write a two-page summary and identify and discuss four points of agreement and disagreement.

Recommended form for writing the college critique
(CD Form #5)

Your name
Course name and number
Professor's name
Due date
Critique: Title and author(s) of the work you are critiquing

(Summarize what the author said.)
   Xxxxxxxxxxxxxxxxxxxxxxxxxxxxxxxxxxxxxxxxxxxxxxxxxxxxxx
xxxxxxxxxxxxxxxxxxxxxxxxxxxxxxxxxxxxxxxxxxxxxxxxxxxxxxxxxx
xxxxxxxxxxxxxxxxxxxxxxxxxxxxxxxxxxxxxxxxxxxxxxxxxxxxxxxxxx
xxxxxxxxxxxxxxxxxxxxxxxxxxxxxxxxxxxxxxxxxxxxxxxxxxxxxxxxxx
xxxxxxxxxxxxxxxxxxxxxxxxxxxxxxxxxxxxxxxxxxxxxxxxxxxxxxxxxx
xxxxxxxxxxxxxxxxxxxxxxxxxxxxxxxxxxxxxxxxxxxxxxxxxxxxxxxxxx
xxxxxxxxxxxxxxxxxxxxxxxxxxxxxxxxxxxxxxxxxxxxxxxxxxxxxxxxxx
xxxxxxxxxxxxxxxxxxxxxxxxxxxxxxxxxxxxxxxxxxxxxxxxxxxxxxxxxx
xxxxxxxxxxxxxxxxxxxxxxxxxxxxxxxxxxxxxxxxxxxxxxxxxxxxxxxxxx
xxxxxxxxxxxxxxxxxxxxxxxxxxxxxxxxxxxxxxxxxxxxxxxxxxxxxxxxxx
xxxxxxxxxxxxxxxxxxxxxxxxxxxxxxxxxxxxxxxxxxxxxxxxxxxxxxxxxx
xxxxxxxxxxxxxxxxxxxxxxxxxxxxxxxxxxxxxxxxxxxxxxxxxxxxxxxx.

   Xxxxxxxxxxxxxxxxxxxxxxxxxxxxxxxxxxxxxxxxxxxxxxxxxxxxxx
xxxxxxxxxxxxxxxxxxxxxxxxxxxxxxxxxxxxxxxxxxxxxxxxxxxxxxxxxx
xxxxxxxxxxxxxxxxxxxxxxxxxxxxxxxxxxxxxxxxxxxxxxxxxxxxxxxxxx
xxxxxxxxxxxxxxxxxxxxxxxxxxxxxxxxxxxxxxxxxxxxxxxxxxxxxxxxxx
xxxxxxxxxxxxxxxxxxxxxxxxxxxxxxxxxxxxxxxxxxxxxxxxxxxxxxxxxx
xxxxxxxxxxxxxxxxxxxxxxxxxxxxxxxxxxxxxxxxxxxxxxxxxxxxxxxxxx
xxxxxxxxxxxxxxxxxxxxxxxxxxxxxxxxxxxxxxxxxxxxxxxxxxxxxxxxxx
xxxxxxxxxxxxxxxxxxxxxxxxxxxxxxxxxxxxxxxxxxxxxxxxxxxxxxxxxx
xxxxxxxxxxxxxxxxxxxxxxxxxxxxxxxxxxxxxxxxxxxxxxxxxxxxxxx.

Quote an idea from the author with which you agree.
(In a paragraph below discuss what it means and why you agree with it.)

Xxxxxxxxxxxxxxxxxxxxxxxxxxxxxxxxxxxxxxxxxxxxxxxxxxxxxxxxxxxxxx
xxxxxxxxxxxxxxxxxxxxxxxxxxxxxxxxxxxxxxxxxxxxxxxxxxxxxxxxxxxxxx
xxxxxxxxxxxxxxxxxxxxxxxxxxxxxxxxxxxxxxxxxxxxxxxxxxxxxxxxxxxxxx
xxxxxxxxxxxxxxxxxxxxxxxxxxxxxxxxxxxxxxxxxxxxxxxxxxxxxxxxxxxxxx
xxxxxxxxxxxxxxxxxxxxxxxxxxxxxxxxxxxxxxxxxxxxxxxxxxxxxxxxxxxxxx
xxxxxxxxxxxxxxxxxxxxxxxxxxxxxxxxxxxxxxxxxxxxxxxxxxxxxxxxxxxxxx
xxxxxxxxxxxxxxxxxxxxxxxxxxxxxxxxxxxxxxxxxxxxxxxxxxxxxxxxxxxxxx
xxxxxxxxxxxxxxxxxxxxxxxxxxxxxxxxxxxxxxxxxxxxxxxxxxxxxxxxxxxxxx
xxxxxxxxxxxxxxxxxxxxxxxxxxxxxxxxxxxxxxxxxxxxxxxxxxxxxxxxxxxxxx
xxxxxxxxxxxxxxxxxxxxxxxxxxxxxxxxxxxxxxxxxxxxxxxxxxxxxxxxxxxxxx
xxxxxxxxxxxxxxxxxxxxxxxxxxxxxxxxxxxxxxxxxxxxxxxxxxxxxxxxxxxxxx
xxxxxxxxxxxxxxxxxxxxxxxxxxxxxxxxxxxxxxxxxxxxxxxxxxxxxxxxxxxxxx
xxxxxxxxxxxxxxxxxxxxxxxxxxxxxxxxxxxxxxxxxxxxxxxxxxxxxxxxxxxxxx
xxxxxxxxxxxxxxxxxxxxxxxxxxxxxxxxxxxxxxxxxxxxxxxxxxxxxxxxxxxxxx
xxxxx.

Quote another idea from the author with which you agree.
(In a paragraph below discuss what it means and why you agree with it.)

Xxxxxxxxxxxxxxxxxxxxxxxxxxxxxxxxxxxxxxxxxxxxxxxxxxxxxxxxxxxxxx
xxxxxxxxxxxxxxxxxxxxxxxxxxxxxxxxxxxxxxxxxxxxxxxxxxxxxxxxxxxxxx
xxxxxxxxxxxxxxxxxxxxxxxxxxxxxxxxxxxxxxxxxxxxxxxxxxxxxxxxxxxxxx
xxxxxxxxxxxxxxxxxxxxxxxxxxxxxxxxxxxxxxxxxxxxxxxxxxxxxxxxxxxxxx
xxxxxxxxxxxxxxxxxxxxxxxxxxxxxxxxxxxxxxxxxxxxxxxxxxxxxxxxxxxxxx
xxxxxxxxxxxxxxxxxxxxxxxxxxxxxxxxxxxxxxxxxxxxxxxxxxxxxxxxxxxxxx
xxxxxxxxxxxxxxxxxxxxxxxxxxxxxxxxxxxxxxxxxxxxxxxxxxxxxxxxxxxxxx
xxxxxxxxxxxxxxxxxxxxxxxxxxxxxxxxxxxxxxxxxxxxxxxxxxxxxxxxxxxxxx
xxxxxxxxxxxxxxxxxxxxxxxxxxxxxxxxxxxxxxxxxxxxxxxxxxxxxxxxxxxxxx
xxxxxxxxxxxxxxxxxxxxxxxxxxxxxxxxxxxxxxxxxxxxxxxxxxxxxxxxxxxxxx
xxxxxxxxxxxxxxxxxxxxxxxxxxxxxxxxxxxxxxxxxxxxxxxxxxxxxxxxxxxxxx
xxxxxxxxxxxxxxxxxxxxxxxxxxxxxxxxxxxxxxxxxxxxxxxxxxxxxxxxxxxxxx
xxxxxxxxxxxxxxxxxxxxxxxxxxxxxxxxxxxxxxxxxxxxxxxxxxxxxxxxxxxxxx
xxxxxxxxxxxxxxxxxxxxxxxxxxxxxxxxxxxxxxxxxxxxxxxxxxxxxxxxxxxxxx
xxxxxxxxxxxxxxxxxxxxxxxxxxxxxxxxxxxxxxxxxxxxxxxxxxxxxxxxxxxxxx
xxxxxxxxxxxxxxxxxxxxxxxxxxxxxxxx.

Quote an idea from the author with which you disagree.
(In a paragraph below discuss what it means and why you disagree with it.)

Xxxxxxxxxxxxxxxxxxxxxxxxxxxxxxxxxxxxxxxxxxxxxxxxxxxxxxxxxxx
xxxxxxxxxxxxxxxxxxxxxxxxxxxxxxxxxxxxxxxxxxxxxxxxxxxxxxxxx
xxxxxxxxxxxxxxxxxxxxxxxxxxxxxxxxxxxxxxxxxxxxxxxxxxxxxxxxx
xxxxxxxxxxxxxxxxxxxxxxxxxxxxxxxxxxxxxxxxxxxxxxxxxxxxxxxxx
xxxxxxxxxxxxxxxxxxxxxxxxxxxxxxxxxxxxxxxxxxxxxxxxxxxxxxxxx
xxxxxxxxxxxxxxxxxxxxxxxxxxxxxxxxxxxxxxxxxxxxxxxxxxxxxxxxx
xxxxxxxxxxxxxxxxxxxxxxxxxxxxxxxxxxxxxxxxxxxxxxxxxxxxxxxxx
xxxxxxxxxxxxxxxxxxxxxxxxxxxxxxxxxxxxxxxxxxxxxxxxxxxxxxxxx
xxxxxxxxxxxxxxxxxxxxxxxxxxxxxxxxxxxxxxxxxxxxxxxxxxxxxxxxx
xxxxxxxxxxxxxxxxxxxxxxxxxxxxxxxxxxxxxxxxxxxxxxxxxxxxxxxxx
xxxxxxxxxxxxxxxxxxxxxxxxxxxxxxxxxxxxxxxxxxxxxxxxxxxxxxxxx
xxxxxxxxxxxxxxxxxxxxxxxxxxxxxxxxxxxxxxxxxxxxxxxxxxxxxxxxx
xxxxxxxxxxxxxxxxxxxxxxxxxxxxxxxxxxxxxxxxxxxxxxxxxxxxxxxxx
xxxxxxxxxxxxxxxxxxxxxxxxxxxxxxxxxxxxxxxxxxxxxxxxxxxxxxxxx
xxxxxxxxxxxxxxxxxxxxxxxxx.

Quote another idea from the author with which you disagree.
(In a paragraph below discuss what it means and why you disagree with it.)

Xxxxxxxxxxxxxxxxxxxxxxxxxxxxxxxxxxxxxxxxxxxxxxxxxxxxxxxxxxx
xxxxxxxxxxxxxxxxxxxxxxxxxxxxxxxxxxxxxxxxxxxxxxxxxxxxxxxxx
xxxxxxxxxxxxxxxxxxxxxxxxxxxxxxxxxxxxxxxxxxxxxxxxxxxxxxxxx
xxxxxxxxxxxxxxxxxxxxxxxxxxxxxxxxxxxxxxxxxxxxxxxxxxxxxxxxx
xxxxxxxxxxxxxxxxxxxxxxxxxxxxxxxxxxxxxxxxxxxxxxxxxxxxxxxxx
xxxxxxxxxxxxxxxxxxxxxxxxxxxxxxxxxxxxxxxxxxxxxxxxxxxxxxxxx
xxxxxxxxxxxxxxxxxxxxxxxxxxxxxxxxxxxxxxxxxxxxxxxxxxxxxxxxx
xxxxxxxxxxxxxxxxxxxxxxxxxxxxxxxxxxxxxxxxxxxxxxxxxxxxxxxxx
xxxxxxxxxxxxxxxxxxxxxxxxxxxxxxxxxxxxxxxxxxxxxxxxxxxxxxxxx
xxxxxxxxxxxxxxxxxxxxxxxxxxxxxxxxxxxxxxxxxxxxxxxxxxxxxxxxx
xxxxxxxxxxxxxxxxxxxxxxxxxxxxxxxxxxxxxxxxxxxxxxxxxxxxxxxxx
xxxxxxxxxxxxxxxxxxxxxxxxxxxxxxxxxxxxxxxxxxxxxxxxxxxxxxxxx
xxxxxxxxxxxxxxxxxxxxxxxxxxxxxxxxxxxxxxxxxxxxxxxxxxxxxxxxx
xxxxxxxxxxxxxxxxxxxxxxxxxxxxxxxxxxxxxxxxxxxxxxx.

Part Seven

Reading on the College Level

How You Can Be a More Effective Reader on the College Level

There are three reading comprehension perspectives that you must understand and apply to be a competent college reader. What did the author say? What does the author mean? How may the author's work apply to the work of others? Too many college students fall short because they believe that understanding a piece of work consists simply of the first perspective. It is more complicated than just understanding what the author said. Let me explain.

What the author said is simply a literal understanding of the work. What, directly, did he or she say first, second, third, and so forth? For example, "Mary arrived late to school and was assigned detention." Literally, what happen to Mary? She was punished because she came to school late. This is a simple, straightforward interpretation of direct language.

What the author means requires you to infer what the author is also implying. As mentioned earlier, you must do this because authors do not communicate using only direct language.

This perspective requires you, as the saying goes, to "read between the lines."

What does the situation of Mary tell you about the school she attends and her past behavior? It tells you that the school is strict about lateness and, for Mary to be assigned detention now, she has probably been late in the past. The author did not specifically mention school policy or Mary's prior behavior, right? No, but it was implied.

The highest critical thinking level of reading is where you are asked to apply one author's work to that of another. This task is made much simpler if you have a complete literal and inferential understanding of the work first. From this, you are in a better position to judge how the two works are the same (compare) and how they are different (contrast).

Remember, when professors assign a reading, they are not asking you to read it once. They are asking you to read it until you completely understand it. With very few exceptions, most of your college reading assignments will require more than one reading. Accept this! You are not going to be tested on a partial understanding of the assigned reading. Read the material until you have it mastered.

Practical Guide for Reading Your College Assignments

- **Survey first:** Look at titles, diagrams, bold type, charts, or any questions that are asked about it by your professor.

- **Topic sentence:** Read the first and last sentence of each paragraph. This is where most topics sentences, the main idea of each paragraph, are located.

- **Read the professor's assignment:** What does the professor want you to do after reading the assignment?

- **Read thoroughly:** Read the material completely through in one sitting if possible. If not, do not put too much time between readings. Pay attention to vocabulary. Have a college-level dictionary nearby and never skip over a word you do not understand.

- **Reread:** Read it more than once if necessary. If you have read the material thoroughly, you should have no difficulty taking your reading notes using the recommended form below and on the next page.

Recommended Reading Form for Taking Your Reading Notes
(CD Form #6)

Date(s) read: _____

Source citation: _____

_____

Part One: Literal understanding (said)

_____

_____

_____

_____

Part Two: Inferences drawn (meant)

_____

_____

_____

_____

Part Three: Application

In what way(s), if any, does this piece compare, contrast, inform, or contradict other related course readings?

_____

_____

_____

_____

Part Four: Personal view

Briefly note if you liked, disliked, agreed with, or disagreed with this piece.

_____

_____

_____

_____

Part Five: The assignment

Do the course assignment. If it was just to read it for the purpose of class discussion, then you are more than prepared to join that discussion.

Part Eight

Your Professor— The Right Approach

How to Approach Your Professor about a Grade

Remember that people like to be asked, and they like to be thanked. Do not forget to ask your professors for help and to thank them when they provide it. Never get in a professor's face about a grade. Diplomacy, not confrontation, gets a grade changed if an honest mistake was made by the professor. Approach the professor by asking, "How can I make this better?" Not, "I think you cheated me on this grade." No professor in the world would ever fail to appreciate and to respond to the first student's approach and respond defensively to the second. In fact, with the first approach, a very common response from professors would be to give the feedback requested and then let you do the assignment again for an averaged grade. (Do not expect this, but do not be surprised if it is offered.) It is all in your approach.

Make certain that you pay attention to how the professor wants his or her assignments prepared. As discussed earlier, process is almost as important as content. Give exactly what is requested and nothing less.

What to Do When You Disagree with Your Professor

No competent, ethical, and professional professors seek to intentionally propagandize his or her students. They do not have a right to expect you to think as they do or to believe in what they believe. College after all is about training you to become an independent thinker. What they do have, however, is a right and a professional obligation to expect you to demonstrate a complete understanding of the course material as they presented it to you.

Do not worry about having a confrontation with your professor over course content differences. It does not matter whether you agree or disagree with the professor. What matters is that on tests and assignments, your obligation as a student is to give back to the professor an understanding of the course material.

Of course, class discussion of course materials with the professor obligates you to comport yourself as you would speaking with anyone else. It is okay to have differences, but it is never okay to be rude. Always be polite and diplomatic. Remember, you are exchanging and discussing points of view or opinion—those of various writers and scholars, those of your professor, those of yourself, and those of your fellow classmates. As I have always told my students, "It's okay to disagree with me. I'm not training a bunch of monkeys."

If you should find yourself in that rare course where the professor neither understands nor appreciates what was presented above, your first duty is to survive. Give back the garbage given to you and move on! Do not get into a professor's face because you will lose.

How and Why You Should Give Your Professor a Course Evaluation

Do not fail to give course evaluations at the end of the semester when requested to do so. Grandma taught us all that "If you have nothing nice to say about a person, say nothing at all." I would add one piece of advice. In the course evaluation, find something nice to say and avoid anything negative not expressed in diplomatic terms.

If you must criticize, certainly be honest and true to yourself. But try to be as positive and as constructive as you can so the course may be improved for students who follow you. Your professor will appreciate the maturity of your approach and as a consequence, seriously consider your constructive advice. Remember that course evaluations are usually distributed to students to fill out at the final exam and it is not uncommon for professors, and their teaching assistants, to read these evaluations before they grade your final exam.

A Final Word

College is easy if you know what you are doing; it is almost impossible if you do not. Read this manual several times and apply its advice to your organization and skills as a college learner. I have eliminated extraneous information that you do not need to know right now. I have given you a highly effective framework for succeeding in college on a high level immediately. You will build on this framework over the course of your college career.

This book is designed to be as practical as a cookbook, and my intention is to have you use it exactly as such. When you want to bake a cake, you open the cookbook to the cake you want and follow the recipe. Likewise, when you need to write your college research paper, open this book to the research paper section and follow the step-by-step recipe. When you need to write your college critique, open this book to the college critique section and follow that step-by-step recipe.

When you want to be a successful college-level writer starting with your very first assignment, turn to the college writing section and follow the detailed instructions. When you need to approach your professor about a grade or are in disagreement with his or her course content views, consult this book to learn how to constructively and correctly approach these matters so that you advance, and not harm your academic career.

This manual offers a great deal of useful advice on how to be a success in college. Take it with you and live its advice. You will not be disappointed. Good luck! I know you will be successful.

Index

Part One: Understanding the Importance of Organization

Importance of process, 1
Importance of organization, 2
College notebook, 3
Class notes, 3
Assigned readings, 4
Grades, 5
College syllabus, 5
Sample college syllabus, 6

Part Two: How to Be Successful in College

Practical advice on how to survive from day to day, 9
Put in the time, 9
Manage your time, 10
Working during the school year, 10
Getting your rest, 10
Missing class, 11
Cutting class because you are unprepared, 11
Do the work, 11
Sit in the front of class, 12
Be an active listener, 12
Speak in every class, 12
Establish a respectful relationship with your professors, 13
Review and revision, 13
Attack your assignments, 14
Reading, 14
Writing, 14
Struggle, 15
Work ethic, 15
Remember who you are, 16
Vital words and what professors mean when they use them, 16
Literal, 16

Implied, 16
Simile, 17
Metaphor, 17
Ambiguous, 17
Appreciation, 18
Polemics, 18
Style manual, 19
Source citation, 19

Part Three: Formal College Writing

Writing standards you must bring to college, 21
Contractions, 21
Personal pronoun "I," 22
The phrase "in my opinion," 22
Use of etc., 22
Grammar and spelling, 22
Pronoun and its antecedent, 22
Tone of your writing, 23
Politeness and writing, 23
Weight of words, 23
Mixing tenses, 23
Avoid common mistakes with confusing words, 24
Its, It's, 24
Their, there, and they're, 25
Than, Then, 25
To, Too, Two, 25
Whose, who's, 25
Important prefixes and suffixes you should remember, 25
Inter-, 25
Intra-, 25
-ism, 26
-ist, 26
Correlative conjunctions, 26

Neither/nor and either/or, 26
Use of numbers, 26
Ordinal numbers, 26

Part Four: How to Write the College Research Paper—Process
What your paper should physically look like, 27
Type size and font, 27
Margins, 27
Justification, 27
Indenting, 27
Block quoting, 28
Source citation, 28
Sources, 28
Page numbering, 28
Title page, 29
Miscellaneous (Plastic covers, pictures, data), 29
Sample title page, 30
Source citation requirements, 31
Sic, 31
Thesis, 32
Organizing your research paper parts, 30
Taking your research notes, 35
Finished appearance of your paper, 36

Part Five: How to Write the College Research Paper—Content
Steps to researching your paper, 37
Steps to writing the content of your paper, 40
Introduction, 40
Step One: The attention step (first paragraph), 41
Step Two: First summary (Second paragraph), 42
Step Three: Need or hook Step (Third paragraph), 42
How long should the introduction be? 42
Body, 43
Conclusion, 43
Final summary, 43
Action step as clincher, 43
Write the introduction last, 43

Write a more effective introduction, 44
Checklist for reviewing the content of your paper, 45

Part Six: Writing the College Critique
The levels of appreciation, 47
Basic, 47
Intellectual, 48
Critical, 48
College critique, 49
Recommended college critique format, 51
Physical appearance of your critique, 51–53

Part Seven: Reading on the College Level
Effective college-level reading, 55
Guide for your college reading assignments, 56
Recommended form for your reading notes, 57–58

Part Eight: Your Professor—The Right Approach
Asking about a grade, 59
Disagreement with professor, 60
Your course evaluation, 61
A final word, 61